MW01170633

A TRUE TRAGEDY

MY 9-11

The Fateful Story of a Mother and Her Daughters Heading to their 9-11

JULIE WILHITE

First Printing: A True Tragedy: My 9-11

Author: Julie Wilhite
© 2021

Cover Art and Design: Eleos Press
Interior Formatting: Eleos Press,
For more information, contact:
moorescott@aol.com

Some of the characters appearing in this work are fictitious. Any resemblance to real persons, living or dead, is purely coincidental.

ISBN-13: 9798704217749

PRINTED IN THE UNITED STATES OF AMERICA

INTRODUCTION

Some of the names have been changed in this book to maintain the dignity and privacy of others.

I have spent the last 30 plus years with plans to write about the tragic events of "My 9-11," experience that almost took the lives of my two daughters and ME at the hands of my husband and their father. I will share some of the most personal, private, horrific, humiliating and embarrassing acts, some that I have never shared before. Acts leading up to 9-11-1989. Twelve years to the day of the real 9-11 attack that took place on US soil. Acts that caused so much shame and feelings of foolishness, a lack of good judgement, and stupidity, injuring my dignity and self-respect.

A lot of tears, joy, pain sadness and many other feelings went into writing this Book. I hope it brings encouragement to whoever reads it.

I was born in 1958 to a farmer and a tall, beautiful blonde. My father was a recovering alcoholic and my mother was a devout Christian and nurse. I am writing this book as an encouragement to other women, and to anyone who finds themselves in a situation that seems hopeless. It is only through my faith in Jesus Christ that my daughters and I are alive today.

I have a lot of God stories that took place after 9-11, miracles that got me through other things that took place after that night. The story didn't end on 9-11.

DEDICATION

This book is dedicated to my precious husband that the Lord has now given me, for showing me what a husband and a father is supposed to be like. For loving, respecting and caring for me and my daughters. For seeing me through all of my struggles in life. Thank you, to the best man I have ever known.

To my two beautiful daughters who had to endure and experience horrific acts at the hands of their father, and became my very best friends from the day they were born. Thank you, girls, for filling that void of friendships that I lost after high school. Love you, girls.

To my parents: thank you, mother, for sharing your faith with me, and all that went with that. Thank you, daddy, for saving our lives. RIP Mom and Dad. See you again one day.

ACKNOWLEDGMENT

To my attorney friend: We always talked about me writing a book. After 30 years, I knew it was now or never. Hard to believe that, over 30 years ago, a scared, beaten-down, hopeless mother of two walked into your office. Thank you for your legal representation, and over 30 years of true friendship.

TABLE OF CONTENTS

THE CHASE

It was one of those dark and eerie nights. Leaves were rustling in the trees. An occasional gust of wind would blow every little bit. You could feel something was about to happen. You knew it wasn't going to be good. Everything seemed mysterious and strange. It was that chill that goes up your spine when you hear a coyote howl. I am already nervous because I have been warned. I know it's going to happen. I just don't know when. My Husband is going to kill me. I feel like it's going to be tonight.

About that time the door burst open and there he was! The chase is on. I run out the door and I am running for my life! It is dark outside. I can barely see my hand in front of my face. I am running and running but he is catching up with me. He is getting closer and closer. I can hardly breathe from the fear of being caught. I am trying to get away, but he is gaining closer and closer. I am looking for a place to hide, but there is no place to hide. I don't want to die, but I know that I am. He told me I was going to.

He catches me. He starts choking me. I can't breathe. I am gasping for breath. I am straining to breathe. I am trying to fight back. I am trying to remove his hands from my neck. I am not able to do so. I am trying to scream, but will anyone hear me...? I am making noises but my screams are not loud. I can't get anything out. I am losing. I can't fight back anymore. About that time my husband is trying to wake me up. It's okay, Julie, you're ok now. You were having another nightmare. But wait—that was not my first husband!

THE BEGINNING

It was a beautiful spring day. The birds were chirping. The flowers were blooming. It couldn't have been a more perfect day—at least that is what my momma said. It was April 21st, 1958 as a matter of fact. That is the day I was born, in a small town in Alabama. My mother was a devout Christian and very smart academically. She would later go back to school and become a nurse. My dad was a farmer. My dad did not finish high school. I think he quit when he was in the 11th grade. My dad was six years older than my mother.

My mother was a beautiful, tall, thin blonde. My dad was extremely handsome. I understand why my mother was interested in my dad. She was six years younger, and this handsome man was interested in her. She was engaged to another guy already. She wanted to date my dad so she broke it off with her boyfriend. She said she broke his heart. He cried for days.

When my mother met my dad, she said she knew he was the one. My dad fought in the Korean War. He was home on leave when they met. They met at this hamburger joint across the road from the local skating rink where everyone hung out. This was in the early 1950s, so there wasn't a lot to do but go to church, roller skating, or a hayride every now and then.

It is easy to picture all that in my mind because that is what we did when I was a kid. I remember going to that same place where they met. It was so cool. It reminded me of the show I use to watch on TV called Happy Days. The church I attended regularly, every so often would go skating for a family night outing. I remember going across the road to the burger joint and having some French Fries one time. The waitress came up to your car window and took your order and they hung that plastic tray on your door with your food on it like they did on the TV show. I only remember doing that one time.

When we went skating my sister and I would share a fountain drink. I am pretty sure we were the only ones who had to share something. We usually got two or three different flavors mixed in the soft drink cup because we couldn't decide on what to get. It was pretty normal back then for my sister and me to share.

There were a few things that my mother was insistent about and one of them was going to the Grand Ole Opry in Nashville Tennessee. I don't remember how many times we went. I know we went several times when I was a child. I know the last time we went I was a teenager because my youngest sister was a little girl. Probably not past the age of 14 or 15. Where the sharing part came in then, is when we went to the opry we had to share. We could share a soft drink, a bag of popcorn or a Goo Goo Cluster. Nashville was famous for the Goo Goo Cluster, so that was what we usually chose—because that was the only time we had access to that candy bar. The Goo Goo Cluster was created in Nashville in 1912, and that was one of the biggest advertisers at the show.

I remember the excitement as a child being on the street with large crowds of people across from the opera house waiting on Dolly Parton and Porter Wagner to arrive. That was huge back then, especially for a little girl in Alabama.

My mother was in the 11th grade when my dad and mom got married. I think they only dated for six months. I am sure it was because my mother wouldn't have done anything inappropriate until she was married, so they went ahead and got married before she finished school. She preached that one thing to me and my sister our entire life. In my mother's eyes sex outside of marriage was the greatest sin a person could commit. My mother was a very godly woman and had high morals that she lived by. She never wavered from what she believed.

A TRUE TRAGEDY: MY 9-11

My dad was shot while he was in the war and that is what brought him home early.

My mom and dad had three daughters: my oldest sister, myself and a younger sister. I was the middle child. My older sister and I were only 22 months apart. My younger sister was almost 12 years younger than me. They were not expecting her, so she was a surprise. When my mother and dad got married, my mother didn't know that dad had a drinking problem. She had never seen that side of him until sometime after they were married in 1954.

My mother's parents were the grandparents that I spent most of my time. My grandmother was what I called a city slicker. She worked public jobs and even had her own café when I was a young teenager.

My granddaddy was who I was close to. He farmed and had a couple of chicken houses. I spent a lot of time with him. I loved him so much. He was such a kind and meek Godly man. My mother said that when she was a young teenage girl that my grandmother was gone a lot late at night working, so it was just my mother and granddaddy at home when she was growing up. She said they spent a lot of lonely nights while my grandmother was at work. My mother was the youngest of three. She had a sister and brother who had already left home, so it was just my mom and granddaddy. My mother's brother joined the military and her sister was a military wife.

I remember spending a lot of time also when I was a child at night with my grandparents, and my grandmother would come home very late. Granddaddy would say she was at her sister's in Birmingham or at work. That never seemed really right to me as a kid, but as an adult I have had other thoughts in my mind.

I remember going to milk the cow with my granddaddy. The cow's name was *Daisy*. He would let me drive his old car around on the farm. It was a small farm and very modest lifestyle. I remember when I would go with my granddaddy to the field to work, we would stop at the end of each row that we were hoeing weeds from and rest, get a drink of water and sometimes half a candy bar, and stomp a few maypops that grew along a fence post. He always had a handkerchief that he would take out of his pocket and wipe the sweat off his brow.

My most favorite thing to do with him was to sit on the porch and kill flies. We got a penny for every fly that we killed. Back then we had a lot of flies. That was one of the things that you were yelled at way back then for, was leaving the door open and letting the flies in. My dad's famous words were "shut the door you are letting the flies in." Not sure where the flies went because these days, we rarely ever have a fly in the house or see a fly unless it's on a dead animal.

My mother grew up a Methodist and went to church regularly. My mother changed to the Baptist faith after she married my dad. Back then after church on Sunday we went to grandmother and granddaddy's house for lunch, my mother's parents. My dad's parents were not church goers. I never saw them go or knew of them going when I was growing up.

We went to the Baptist Church where my dad's oldest brother was the song director, and my mother played the piano. My dad's oldest brother and his wife had a beautiful home with a swimming pool and a small plane that my uncle flew. My aunt raised chickens also, and my uncle had a really good job. My aunt was the epitome of class. I thought of her as equal to Jackie Kennedy. Her house and yard were perfect. She was an awesome decorator and had the means to do it. I think that is what made me want to decorate my home and yard after I was grown. I never had the means to just go buy anything, but I was able to create it. My mother was an awesome seamstress and could make us beautiful dresses out of fabric that she could afford when we were little. She could also make professionally made drapes. She taught me how to sew, but I would never take the time to do all that stuff she could do. I would always cut corners. Not enough patience to do it correctly. I wanted to hurry up and get it done. I was really good at hiding all my flaws.

My mother didn't ever miss church. As the ole saying goes, we were there every time the door was open. My mother's faith in God was as strong as it gets. My faith in Jesus is what got me through life, and I owe that to my mother. I will never forget when I was a young girl the old-time revivals that lasted a week or two.

I will tell you how dedicated my mother was. One time on Sunday morning the car would not start. My dad was not home for some reason. We were not going to miss church. My mother got the tractor out of the shed. She climbed up on the tractor in one of those tight skirts, and my sister and I had to stand on the back of the tractor all the way to church. Now we lived on a dirt road, so you can picture that in your mind. My sister and I were old enough to be very embarrassed when we arrived.

I remember when they installed the first bathroom at the church. We use to go to the outhouse to the bathroom. I always remember having an indoor bathroom growing up at our house. We didn't have an air conditioner in our home until I was in about the 10th grade in high school. It was a window unit. The only good thing about not having an air conditioner was the windows were raised to let in hopefully a cool breeze. If, by any chance, it happened to rain during the night that was the best sleep a person could ever experience. The cool breeze blowing in the window and listening to the rain. I can still picture in my mind the curtains blowing from the window. The bad thing about having to raise our windows was we lived on a dirt road and every time a car came down the road all the dust came in the house. We had to dust the furniture often. The only heat we had was two space heaters for the entire house. I remember getting up for school, and my sister and I would huddle close together by the heater to get warm before school.

My dad was one of 8 children. He was right in the middle. He was number 4. My Papa, my dad's father was interested in only one thing and that was work. My dad was the same way. I have been the same way most of my life. The difference in me is work didn't interfere with my family life. My granny told me that my dad and one of his other brothers took the brunt of all the whippings. According to another family member my dad was whipped very badly a lot. Today's standards would be considered child abuse if you whipped your children like that now. She told me that they would have knots on their legs as big as the size of an egg when they got a whipping.

My dad told me they nearly starved to death when my Papa went to prison. He said that they only had a cold piece of corn bread and water before school at times. He said that they only got one pair of shoes a year and if they wore them out before winter, they would go barefooted. He told me they were so poor that they had to carry their lunch to school in a whiskey bottle and wrap their cornbread or whatever they were eating up in a newspaper. Everyone else had a brown paper bag to carry their lunch in. He said they would hide their lunch in a tree and eat it on the way home so they wouldn't be made fun of. Everyone made fun of them because their dad was in prison.

The only thing that I know about my Papa going to prison, according to my dad was: one night my Papa, his dad, and another family member were drinking and playing cards and gambling. Some reason a fight broke out and a man was killed. My Papa and his dad and this other man were accused and went to prison. According to Public Record, he was 33 or 34-years-old. According to Public Record, it was manslaughter, first degree. My Papa got five years. This was somewhere around 1937. That would have made my dad around seven or eight-years-old. According to my dad my Papa was let out of prison after two years to come home and take care of his family. My dad told me that they did get into a fight and that my Papa said that he did not kill him.

That is really all that I have ever been told about that. My granny told me some of it, and my dad told me some of it. I am not sure if all that I just said happened that way. That is just what I was told. A family member told me that when she was married into the family that was never talked about, and it was never to be mentioned around the family.

My Papa was what I would consider a millionaire when he passed away. Of course, their lifestyle was very simple. Nothing fancy or impressive except for the farm and all of his equipment. The first house that they lived in, until I was about eight, was old and awful looking. It was nothing nice at all, not anything you would want to live in. The kitchen and bathroom were horrible. They built a nice modest brick house after that.

I was told he owned around 400 acres of land in all. He had many head of cattle, some rental property, and chicken houses. He had a lot of pigs. I used to take the slop bucket from their house to the pig pen and fed it to the pigs. If you don't know what a slop bucket was, it is all the food like potato peelings, rotten food etc., and put into a bucket. That is what pigs eat, it is garbage.

He even had a potato house. It was a block building where he stored all of the potatoes that we had dug and picked up. It was dark and very cool in there. That kept the potatoes fresh. We would separate them by size and get rid of the bad ones. I know that my sister, a couple of aunts and a cousin or two, and I picked up 700 bushels of potatoes once—and that was not all of them. That was just one day's work. The potatoes were lying on the ground as far as my eyes could see.

I know one thing that I did that a lot of people my age never did back then was I picked a lot of cotton at my Papa's farm when I was a kid. That was some back breaking stuff, let me tell you. I worked really hard because at the end of the day you didn't want to be the one with the least amount of cotton picked when you weighted in. My Papa finally purchased a cotton-picker. I was so excited because I wasn't going to have to pick cotton anymore. The bad part about it was we had to go behind the cotton picker and pick up all the cotton that fell on the ground. That was just as hard because we had to bend over all the way to the ground and that was more backbreaking than before.

My dad said Papa started buying up property after he got out of prison. I hated to go over there and work. It was worse than working on the farm at home. I remember one time that his tractor broke down and while he was repairing it, instead of getting a break, I had to go to the house and iron his overalls. They were hard as a rock. They had starch on them and had hung out on the line to dry. No putting them in the dryer like we do today. It was all I could do to keep from crying. However, I had to do it. I was scared not too. He would have never said anything to me, but I wasn't going to push my luck and find out. I would have been in more trouble at home if I had not of finished my work.

Back then you did what you were told. You didn't argue with anyone. Papa was very cold. He was what

I called a lot of those people back in those days. A hard ole soul. I guess it was a lot of the things that they had experienced in their life. Life was tough back then. My granny was a very sweet lady but not very maternal, not toward us anyway. I only remember Papa and Granny coming to my house one time when I was a kid. The only reason was Papa was taking Granny to see her sister and our house was on the way.

For some reason all of my daddy's siblings have done very well financially before and after my Papa passed away except for my dad. He always lost everything we had more than one time. I realize now that a lot of the arguments that my parents had were from my mother trying to manage the money, because my dad overspent and had nothing to show for it. My dad just didn't have any sense of money. He was unable to manage money. I don't think he could help it. My dad passed away owing for his farm that he had refinanced more than once. I wasn't able to sell enough of his personal property to save the farm.

A lot of the way my dad was had to do with how he was raised. I guess he was the "black sheep" in his dad's eyes, and my dad must have not measured up. One thing my dad did was tell us he loved us every night when we went to bed. Also, if we wanted a drink of water or a cracker, he would let us have it. I think he did that because he went to bed hungry when he was a kid so he wasn't going to let us be hungry. At least, that is what my mother told me, and he was never told he was loved by his parents.

THE FARM

The farm that I grew up on, we moved to when I was two. My very first memories were playing on the carport. The house we moved from didn't have an indoor bathroom and my mother said that the walls had cracks wide enough between the boards that when it snowed in the winter time it would come inside the house. I am glad I was too little to remember that.

Our new house was very plain and very small but it wasn't bad. We had sheet rock walls and hardwood floors. We had brown kitchen appliances. That was what was in style at that time. Our bathroom was very small, but it was clean and the tub was your normal shower and tub combination. The only stain was in the tub where the water came out of the faucet because we had well water. We had to scrub that stain all the time to keep it from being there. The well water would turn all of your white clothes yellow when you washed them. My mother didn't have the fanciest things, but she kept everything super clean. She would borrow an electric buffer that belonged to these people that we went to church with, every so often to buff the hardwood floors. Otherwise, my sister and I had to buff them with a towel the best that we could. We would stand on the towel and do "The Twist" to music so we didn't have to get on our hands and knees.

When I was a child, we had all the childhood diseases that you had back then. Big red measles, Chicken Pox, Mumps, etc. When I got the Mumps, my mother got them also and they fell on her (that's what they called it back then) and she was hospitalized. She was in pretty bad shape. When we got sick, we would have fever up to 104 because we didn't have medicine like we do today. When we had the flu or something that caused chest congestion, we would heat cloths by one of only two three-stack heaters in our entire house that we had to stay warm by. We would rub our chest with salve and put those hot cloths on our chest so we could breathe.

I remember having the flu and couldn't hold my head up. I was so sick, that my mother was afraid to leave me at the house by myself. She carried me to the chicken house with her while she fed chickens and I had to sit on a bucket. I don't know how I sat there. We had what you call a truck farm. We grew vegetables and we raised chickens. We had two chicken houses that housed about 20,000 chickens per house. I think now a Chicken house will house about 40,000 per house. Nowadays, everything is pushbutton. Big chicken house farmers now, have someone to see after their chicken houses. Back then we had to hand feed them, fill up hundreds of water jugs twice a day and a whole number of other things that went along with raising chickens. We raised what you call, *Broilers*. That meant we got them as new born baby chicks and kept them for eight weeks. Then the chicken catching crews would come catch them and take them to the chicken plant where the next steps were taken to get them ready to sell in the grocery stores. In 2015, chickens (broilers) were # 1 in the state in agricultural—raking in 3.6 billion dollars in cash receipts. The top commodity in Alabama ranked # 2 in the US.

My oldest sister and I had to work extremely hard on the farm. We were 22 months apart and very close. In the summer months along with taking care of the chicken houses, we worked from sun up to sun down out in the fields. There was no time for play. We played very little. We incorporated play in with our work. One way we did it, was right before we sold a bunch of chickens, we would catch about 20 chickens out of a chicken house. My mother would ring their necks and skin them. There would be all these headless chickens flopping around all over the yard. That's where my sister and I came in. We would wash the chickens, cut them up and put them in freezer bags. Back then it took a bunch of chickens eight weeks to produce. Way more time than it does today. Almost everything we ate was produced on the farm.

The way we made play time out of chores was, before we cut the chickens up, we would take these headless chickens and pretend we were having a battle with them. We would fight with their wings and legs. I know it sounds morbid, but we were just kids. I always wanted a Barbie doll with bendable legs and real hair. I never got one. I got a plastic one from the dime store that did nothing. When we shucked the corn for dinner, or to put in the freezer we took the silks from the corn cob and taped onto our ball headed plastic dolls head and pretended it was hair. I remember that I got one baby doll. I did get paper dolls. I remember playing with paper dolls the most. I would get in my bedroom closet and dump all the paper dolls out on the floor, and play until I was told differently. I loved playing with my paper dolls.

I also remember making homemade ice cream. One of us would have to sit on the churn while the other turned the handle. We would put a towel on the ice cream churn so our rear end would not get wet from the cold ice. I don't know which was the worst—sitting on the ice cream churn and freezing your butt off or turning the handle until you thought your arm was going to fall off. "Oh my. What a treat." Homemade ice cream is still a treat today, but we have an electric churn.

When my kids or grand kids would complain about something, I would tell them my sob story: when I was in the 11th grade in high school, I had to get up at 4:00 a.m. and feed two houses of chickens before I went to school every day. Even when school started back in the fall, my sister and I would be up sometimes until 2:00 in the morning—packing produce for my dad to take to the farmers' market to sell. I fell asleep in school a lot.

Back then we took our vegetables to the farmers' market in the big city in Alabama, about 50-60 miles south of where we lived. We would be there all night long, and sleep on the back of the pickup truck. It was fun for me. I enjoyed selling the produce. That was probably the most enjoyable thing to do on the farm, was going to the farmers' market. We would walk all over that place. You can't do that anymore. The crime is too bad. You would be robbed or killed today if you did it like we did back then. It's more commercial now. You sell mostly to someone who has businesses or companies that sell to grocery stores. Back then the community came out to buy your vegetables and you got to meet the people.

I remember the first time I saw a pregnant lady. It happened to be at the market. I questioned what I was seeing. My dad told me that she swallowed a watermelon seed and she grew a watermelon in her stomach. I remember my sister and I were so afraid after he told us that. We were afraid that we would swallow a watermelon seed every time we ate a watermelon and we would start growing a watermelon in our stomach. That didn't go on to long before we learned the truth.

A TRUE TRAGEDY: MY 9-11

Had it not been for my mother, my sister and I would not have gotten to do anything but work. I got to be a majorette; we were in the band. She tried starting us taking piano lessons, but every time we tried to take them, we had to quit because it interfered with work. We did go to the beach every summer for a weekend. I love the beach. The beach is my most favorite thing to do in the world. We stayed in what we call now a roach motel. Most all of them have been torn down now. Now it is mostly high-rise condos.

My dad hired people to work on the farm from time to time. He hired this guy that was in my class at school.   He told me that he was shocked to see my sister and me on top of the chicken house painting black tar on top of the tin. Work that grown men do. That is like what my sister and I had to do. My dad was hard on me and my sister. That is all my dad knew. That is how he grew up. My dad said to me one time that "all that hard work didn't hurt you." I told him, "Yes—it did a little bit."

The part that hurt me is that for a long time I couldn't take time to smell the roses my own self. All I do is work. I can't relax. My mind races all the time about what I am going to do next. Everything has to be done. I can't watch anything on TV all the way through, I have to get up and start doing something else. I am way better than I used to be. The thing that all that work helped me to do was to be able to work two fulltime jobs, a part-time job, and take care of my two daughters when we were going through all that we went through. It did teach me to work for what I have. I never had to ask anyone for anything except a job. The one thing that I regret is that I didn't get a better education and all these years I could have worked one job for the same amount of money that I worked two or three jobs.

There were a lot of embarrassing times on the farm, like when I had a date with this guy. He arrived to pick me up, but we were not finished working in the field, so he had to sit there and wait on me to get finished working. I had to come to the house and get ready before going on the date. He sat there waiting on me for about an hour and a half. I was humiliated to say the least.

The bad part of the entire incident was that I had to walk in front of him with this stupid aircraft cap on my head that I would wear in the chicken house to keep the chicken house smell from staying in my hair. When you work in a chicken house every day, the chicken smell will stay in your hair no matter how many times that you wash it, if you do not cover your head every time you go in there. No makeup on, I was dirty, and smelt horrible. There was no way around it. We had two doors—a front door and a back door. He was sitting in the living room. Either way I went in the house I had to walk past him to get to the bathroom and the bedroom to get ready. I don't recall us ever going out again. If that wasn't scary enough for him, having to sit there and talk to my mother for an hour and a half on a first date would have made me not ever want to come back. I have often wondered whatever happened to him.

Another time was, when my best friend in high school would come to spend the night at my house, sometimes I had work to do, I had to work no matter whether I had company or not. I remember I had to hand-wash these gallon jugs by hand that we filled up with water that the baby chickens drank out of. She sat out there and talked to me while I worked. I remember her saying that she couldn't believe that I didn't cuss. I guess she thought that all the things that I had to do on the farm; I would have been a tobacco chewing backward cussing hillbilly. However, I spent the night with her way more than she did me.

We met in the 10th grade. She walked into algebra class and that was the first time I had ever seen her. She had come from California. Her dad was retiring from the military. Her dad's family was from Alabama. As a matter of fact, her dad's sister was also my aunt who was married to one of my dad's brothers. Such a small world. It gets even smaller as the story goes.

A TRUE TRAGEDY: MY 9-11

I am grateful for my parents and my upbringing even though a lot of things caused me to make some very stupid decisions. I owe everything to my mother. She never wavered from what she believed. No matter if everyone was doing it and society had conformed to whatever that everyone was doing at the time. Not my mother, if it was wrong 100 years ago, it was wrong now.

I don't want to sound disrespectful toward my parents in anyway when I say the things that I do in this book. I am sure they did the best that they could. Times were hard back then for a lot of people. This is who I am. I have had to overcome a lot of things. Some things I have not overcome and probably never will in this life.

My dad was an alcoholic. He didn't drink all the time, but when he did it was a doozy. He is what I called a binge drinker. He was non-functioning when he got drunk. We would say he was "on a drunk." He would stay drunk for about a week or two when he got drunk. There are people that can drink and people that cannot. When my dad drank, he didn't stop. He would be out of his mind. There was no talking or reasoning with him. There were a lot of funny stories and some not so funny. This was not funny at the time but, to tell it now, at least we can laugh about it.

This particular day we were not in the field working, just my dad. He was on the tractor plowing. My mother always prepared a big lunch each day. Everything we had to eat we grew on the farm. Lunch time was 12 noon. My mother waited and waited and my dad didn't show up. Finally, my mother went to the field to see what was wrong. She found the tractor sitting in the middle of the field, but no dad. The tractor was still running. He didn't even cut it off. He came home a week later. He had pulled a drunk. That is what we called it back then. One of his drinking buddies had stopped by and that's all it took. It wasn't hard to get my dad to go off with him and get some alcohol. It wasn't as easy to find someone back then like it is now either.

A TRUE TRAGEDY: MY 9-11

We only had a landline telephone that you shared with two other families in your community. It was called a party-line. You would try to listen to your neighbor's conversations, and they would yours, also. But, most of the time, they could tell you were eavesdropping. I can't image people having to share a phone line with your own family members, not to mention your neighbors. Road rage would be minor compared to neighbor rage these days.

A not-so-funny time was when my dad went to farmers' market and sold all of the produce we had gathered. He stopped at some hole in the wall bar on the way home. Someone spiked his alcohol and he woke up by a creek in the woods beaten, robbed and left for dead. I am sure that money was to pay bills. My sister took on the role as caretaker when my dad drank. I was afraid of daddy when he got drunk.

My sister on the other hand would pet him; put wet cloths on his head. She would get him tomato juice when he would be sick and have a hangover. I was so afraid when Daddy got drunk that my legs would nearly shake off my body. I would go and hide in my bedroom. Daddy would always want to dance to the Righteous Brothers' music when he got drunk. I hated that! It was so sad to see my dad when he was in that condition because a lot of times he would cry, especially when he played the Righteous Brothers music.

One time, when my sister was five, and I was three years old, my mother worked at the cigar plant. She worked 2nd shift. When she came home one night about midnight, all she could see was the top of my sister's head sitting in the cab of the pickup truck. I can't image the fear that overcame her. We should have been in the bed asleep. As she approached the truck, she saw that my dad was passed out drunk. My sister was holding me rocking me to sleep. Of course, we don't remember any of that. I have no idea where we had been and how we made it home.

The last major drinking episode that daddy had before he quit drinking was when I was 14. We had been up all night, driving him around to people's houses. That's what he would want to do most of the time when he got drunk. We did it because my mother didn't want him to get in the car and kill himself or someone else. So, we had to drive him around. I had on a pair of white denim jeans that day. Sometime during the ordeal daddy got mad about something and slung a cup of coffee out the window. I was in the back seat and it landed on me, all over my white jeans. Daylight had arrived and it was time for school to start. By now daddy had passed out and mother was not going to wake him up and get him going again, so she dropped us off at school before going home. Being a teenage girl, going to school with coffee all over the front of your white pants and everyone wanting to know what happened, was humiliating. That is about the time that my dad quit drinking.

By this time my younger sister had been born. She was about two when Daddy quit drinking. Mother had had enough. She was not going to raise her like that. My mother had my dad committed to a mental hospital. My dad begged to come home. He swore that he would never drink again. Mother got him out and of course, and after a short period of time he relapsed. Mother packed us up and left. That is when he knew that she meant business and he started to (AA) Alcoholics Anonymous. My dad quit drinking after that. (My oldest sister also became an Alcoholic after she finished high school).

This was about the time in my life that I felt God calling me to be a missionary. I had been to Athens State College with my youth group from church. We were there to hear Nicky Cruz, a former gang leader in New York City, talk about his life. There was a movie made about his life called the Cross and Switch Blade. I knew that night that I was supposed to be a missionary. I will never forget being in that gym listening to him speak, when all of a sudden, they announced that we had a bomb threat. I was on the top row of the gym. I thought we would never get out of there. I thought any minute I would blow up. We got outside waiting to see what was going to happen. I remember being so disappointed. I had already seen the movie and wanted to hear what he had to say. Nicky Cruz decided to go on with the crusade outside. That was the best thing that could have happened. The building didn't blow up and all those college students that didn't go to the crusade were hanging out their dorm windows listening. I am sure there were lives that were changed. Mine certainly changed. I always thought of that verse in the Bible, Genesis 50:20. What he meant for evil, God meant for good. Someone wanted to stop the crusade from happening, but it didn't work.

When I was in the 11th grade, I started dating this guy named Clay that was in our class at school. I really liked him a lot. I guess he didn't like me as much as I did him. He broke up with me. Clay was friends with J C. My friend that I shared a little bit about earlier that came from California went out on a date with J C a couple of times and I went out with Clay. She didn't really like J C and didn't want to go out with him anymore. She was the smart one. Our Junior Senior Prom was coming up. I didn't have a date anymore, since Clay had broken up with me. My friend and her date fixed me up with this guy that he knew from the University. The entire night of the prom, my best friend kept trying to get me to swap dates with her. I really wanted to because I was more interested in her date. There was one problem. I was taller than her date and I was not dancing with someone that was shorter than I was. I already had to wear flat shoes so I wouldn't be taller than the guy I was already with. After the prom was over, they carried me home first; all I know is my date carried her home, and they have been together ever since. My friend and I never hung out again after that night. I never knew why. I still wanted to be friends. I was devastated over the end of our friendship.

So, J. C. asked me out. My dad wouldn't let me go out with him. I begged him to let me go. I don't know why I wanted to go out with him. I didn't even like him. I really think it was being upset over losing my best friend and Clay, the guy I really liked. My decision after that was the biggest mistake I have ever made. It changed my life forever. My dad knew what kind of boy he was. My mother was the one who talked my dad into letting me go. That within its self is still a shock today. I don't know why my mother did that.

I think when I started dating him that people looked at me differently. I think that is one of the reasons why my best friend didn't talk to me anymore. It's kind of like who you hang around with sometimes can give you a bad reputation even though you don't do the things that they do. I don't know what I was expecting to become of this relationship. I don't know why I allowed him to treat me with such disrespect. I thought that I thought more of myself than to just go along for the ride. When I think back now, I was probably looked at by my peers a notch or two below of how I considered myself up to that point. I am sure things were said about me that weren't true. I was too young and naive to understand what lay ahead.

My best friend was not my best friend anymore. She was in a serious relationship and was going to marry her boyfriend. Even though I was extremely close to my sister we didn't do much together in high school except when we went riding around with friends after church on Sunday night. That was some of the best times in my life, was with my friends at church. We would have so much fun. My sister and I spent a lot of time together after high school.

My mother used to make me go on double dates with my sister. She thought that would make her not do anything she wasn't supposed to. How wrong she was. I will never forget my sister was going to a Kiss concert with this guy. They were going with the guy's brother and his wife. When they arrived to pick my sister up, my mother didn't like the way they looked. The guys had long hair and looked like hippies. My mother was freaking out. She had this idea that it was not a good idea for her to be with a married couple either. I think she thought that they might not care what they did. Basically, she was so afraid that we would do something before marriage and she was going to prevent that at all cost.

The only way that she was going to let her go was if I went with them. I didn't want to go. I begged and pleaded not to go. You see my sister would do what she wanted to—regardless of whether I was with her or not. My mother just didn't have any idea of the danger that she put me in by making me go. When we got to Huntsville Ala, to watch the concert, we had to park several blocks away. It was dark and they ran off and left me. They didn't want to be late for the concert. I remember running as fast as I could to get to the coliseum. Anything could have happened to me. I had no idea where they were. I found my seat. I am only 15 or 16 and extremely upset. I was sitting there waiting for the concert to start and wanting the night to hurry and be over. The lights went out for Kiss to come on stage, and a different light appeared. The marijuana was flowing. It looked like a gigantic Christmas tree lit up. I was sure I was going to jail. I was afraid that they would think I was a part of that and was going to be arrested.

I think back on that experience and realized nobody cared that all those people were smoking pot. This was the 70's and marijuana, hip-hugger blue jeans, bare feet and halter tops were what most people were doing. I never did smoke marijuana. I was in the car with people riding around who did and tried to talk me into it, but I wouldn't do it. I did smoke cigarettes, something that I am not proud to say that I did. I probably smoked for about five years. The way that I quit was when a lady that I went to church with saw me light one up at the store one day in my car. She confronted me about how shocked she was, and what a bad influence that would have on others. I went home and put them down and never picked them up again.

I smoked over two packs a day, so it wasn't easy. I prayed and asked God to take this away from me. I was in the bed sick for about a week. I had an out-of-body experience. I guess it was like a person having hallucinations. I thought that Jesus and Satan were standing there, talking to me. Satan would tell me to go ahead and smoke, that Jesus said it was ok. It was a rough week. God answered my prayer. To this day I cannot be around cigarette smoke. I can't breathe; my eyes will swell up and pour tears like I am crying. That was over 37 years ago.

Another time that my mother made me go on a date with my sister was to the drive-in movie. Really!!! How am I supposed to make sure that nothing happened to my sister? I was the one that was almost raped. The guy that I was with was in college. He tried to force himself on me in the back seat of the car. He was a huge, muscled-up guy. He pushed me down and I couldn't push him off. He had my pants undone and my shirt completely undone, while I continued to push him off. He obviously had never been turned down very much, especially by a young 16-year-old high school girl. He quit trying to force himself on me and I got out of the car humiliated and held my shirt and pants together, while I made it to the bathroom. I stayed in the bathroom for a little while trying to figure out what to do next.

I asked him to take me home. He cursed me all the way home, calling me every kind of ugly name and using the F-word to do it. I arrived home and told my mother what had happened. There was no way around it. My mother always waited up for us. A lot of my friends' parents didn't do that. I would advise every parent to wait up on their teenagers—that way, you know what kind of shape they are in when they get home. My mother told my dad what had happened. I begged her not to, but she did anyway. My dad asked me some questions and found out he went to the same college that my prom date went to. I think they shared the same dorm. He told my dad that the guy had anger management problems. They had seen him put his fist through the wall before at college.

My dad found out that he knew the guy's mother. I came home from majorette practice one night. He and his mother were there sitting in our living room. I had no idea what was going on. My dad said that he was there to apologize. He did all but apologize. By the time his mother got through with me I could hardly hold back the tears. She asked me all kinds of questions, and blamed me for all of it. Kind of like how society does today. Somehow, it's your fault, no responsibility on the guy's part. The problem was very clear. He was a spoiled brat who was a mommy's boy who was never made to be responsible for his own actions. His mother made it out to be like he was this college guy that was not interested in me, and I was this young teenage girl trying to get revenge because he wasn't interested. According to her I really wanted it but he wouldn't give me the time of day.

My dad asked them to leave. My mother apologized to me for even saying anything seeing how things turned out. This guy married and had a daughter. I have often wondered how things turned out for her. These two incidents that I have told you might make my sister sound bad, but my sister and I were very close and she had lots of problems in her life. She would give you the shirt off her back and do anything in the world for you. She was a very selfless person. Everyone loved her. Her entire life she had very low self-esteem.

I never thought I had low self-esteem. Maybe I did. Like I said about myself, if everyone was doing it and I didn't want to, I didn't care what anyone thought. I didn't have peer pressure. I am still that way today. If I think it is wrong, I could care less what you say or think about me. I guess I get some of that from my mother. The only thing is she was a little extreme with some of her beliefs.

One of the things we did every year was to go to the beach. We went for one weekend out of the year on a vacation to Panama City Beach Florida. We always had worn a one-piece swim suite. I was in my preteens because that was about the time that my younger sister that was an accident was born. My older sister and I wanted to wear a two-piece swimsuit because that was the new style. My mother was not going to let us wear a two-piece, because she was not going to let us show our belly buttons. My mother was so old fashioned that she made us a homemade swim suite out of this blue and white polyester fabric so that she could make the bottoms come up high enough so our belly button wouldn't show. By the time the hip huger jeans and halter tops came out, my mother was over the belly button not showing.

It's hard to believe but back then the gas was 25 cents a gallon. I guess that was a lot back then. We ate out at a restaurant one time at the beach; my mother cooked all the rest of the food that we ate. We stopped along the way down and back from the beach trip at a rest stop or picnic area, and ate homemade ham and tomato sandwiches. We stayed in a cheap roach motel and we had to earn our own money to spend at the amusement park. I remember using the money that I had earned to spend at the beach and I would pay a little extra for my ticket to

JULIE WILHITE

ride the roller coaster as many times as I wanted and I would never get off. I would ride over and over as long as I could. That's just the way things were back then. It prepared me for life—especially the life I was about to face.

So, I went out with J. C., but going out with him was riding around, hanging out looking for a party somewhere. We never really went out on a real date. Not sure what my problem was continuing to go out with him. I still to this day touch my forehead to see if I have a fever and was delirious. Of course, he always tried to force himself on me, and I was never going to do that before marriage. Things happened that I did not intend to let happen and, at this point, I felt I had to get married. According to how my mother thought, I was doomed for hell. She never said that but, to her, that was the ultimate sin, the worst thing you could do. I think she thought that she could scare me into not doing anything. I was not even allowed to wear a tampon, because my mother said that my husband would think I was not a virgin when we got married.

THE HONEYMOON

We got married April 10, 1976 right before graduation. We were married at the church that I had been going to since I was 12 years old. A church that my mother helped start. That church is still going strong today.

We had a very simple wedding. About as simple as you can get. The flowers at the front of the church were two ferns. The church was packed. Our classmates were there. It was kind of like everyone was there to see if this really happened or not.

We went to Huntsville on our Honeymoon. When we got to the hotel, he opens the door, pushed me down on the floor. It was very disrespectful. The door was not even shut. Not what I envisioned a honeymoon to be like. I felt very weird. He left after that and left me alone for the rest of the night. You might ask, "Why did you stay at this point?" Some of it was pride, I guess. "I told you so," by everyone. "It won't last," everyone said. We were always told that "You made your bed; you lay in it." Divorce was not even in the equation in my mother's eyes. I wanted to be married. I always thought things would be different. I have always wondered where did he go all night. I have some thoughts, but why would he do that?

The next night we went to the restaurant that was at the hotel. I remember that we had on jeans, not dressed up. He was 18; I was 17 just a few days till my 18th birthday. When I think back now, I seemed mature, but really, I wasn't. I was still like a child. I had always been told what to do, so I continued to do what I was told and didn't ask questions.

I am pretty sure there was a dress code, because they told us that there were no tables available. I saw a lot of empty tables. I guess the only thing that I had on that met the dress code was my shoes. I forgot my shoes, and wore the silver high heels that I got married in. It looked pretty ridiculous. "Nothing fairy tale about any of this." We had fast food and ate it in the room.

We moved in with his parents. He brought me home to his parents' house after our honeymoon and then he left and was gone for about two or three days. I will always believe from day one that he was always cheating, and he was.

GRADUATION

It was time for our graduation baccalaureate service. After we came home, J. C. dropped me off at his parents' and left. He would not take me with him. This was our senior year. I wanted to be with friends too, just like he did and everybody else did. I went looking for him. He got word that I was looking for him. He came back home and that was the first time that he hit me. He got in my face pointing his finger at me and told me that I had better never ever come looking for him again. I had no idea what to do. I had only been married for a couple of weeks and I found myself in a situation that I had not been in before and didn't know what to do.

Of course, I wasn't going to say anything to my parents or anyone for that matter. I was too afraid to, because of what he might do and I had no idea what my dad would do. Also, I was embarrassed and humiliated. Helplessness, fear, low self-esteem self-blame, anxiety and depression are starting to set in.

Everyone had already said it wouldn't last. I was not allowed to hang out with any of my friends anymore. I know now what was going on. He wanted to still live a single life and be married too. I was his property. I belonged to him. I am sure he had girlfriends on the side and he couldn't do that if I was around. That is why our entire marriage if he took me somewhere with him, he would get mad at me for acting normal, all I had to do was say the wrong thing and he would get violent and take me home. That was so he could be with someone else I guess and party without me like a single person. About the only person that I had was my mother. My sister was doing her thing, so I didn't have her to hang around at the time. My sister had started drinking a lot and she was in nursing school at the time.

My senior year in high school my parents built a restaurant. They named it after my mother and grandmother's name. The restaurant specialized in home cooking. Almost everything we served was homemade. We would start the day at the restaurant around 4am making homemade biscuits and homemade donuts. We moved from J. C.'s parents to my parent's farm to raise chickens. I would be taking care of the chickens as well as working in the restaurant. That was laughable; I was the only one going to be doing the work in the chicken house. J. C. was not going to be tied down to that. He had never had to do that kind of work anyway. It was not in him to work very hard anyway. He always paid to have everything done.

My parents had built a house when they built the restaurant, and had moved from the farm. I was supposed to take care of the chickens. Taking care of the chickens would be our rent money for living there. That didn't last long before my dad and J. C. had words. I knew it was just a matter of time before my dad would make him mad. It was something over cleaning out the chicken house before the next bunch came in. That was something you were supposed to do. I think he was going to try and scatter new shavings on top without cleaning out the old chicken manure.

I am pretty sure he was bootlegging while we were living at my parent's farm because my mom came over there with her Bible to show him the scripture. I told her not to do that but she did anyway. Someone had told my parents what was going on. That was the first I had learned of that. My parents had to tell me that he was bootlegging on their property. Stupid me didn't even know. He held that against her the rest of our married life. An example would be: every time she said or did something he didn't like, he wouldn't let the girls or me see them for an extended period of time. He did the same thing to his own mother and sister if they wouldn't do what he wanted. They always thought I was the one that just wouldn't let the girls come over. I was too afraid to say anything to anyone. So, everyone just thought it was me. One time, my mother came over to have lunch with me after church. He punished her for preaching from the Bible to him for the past several years: when she sat down at the table to eat, he got up and left.

He was mad at his sister for breaking up with the guy she was engaged to and marrying someone else. She had asked for my oldest daughter to be her flower girl at her wedding. I was sure he wouldn't let her, because that was how he played his mind-games when you did something he didn't like. So I just said, "Okay," and hoped for the best. He was supposed to be out of town on a trip. I was just going to let her be the flower girl and face the consequences later. I guess I thought he would not find out. I don't know what I was thinking. I wasn't thinking. He came home for whatever reason; he was supposed to be gone. I asked him if we could go to the wedding and of course the answer was no. I had to tell him then that she was supposed to be the flower girl. This was the day of the wedding. There was a big falling out over that.

Back to working in the chicken house. While working in the chicken house, my wedding rings fell out of my pocket and the chickens ate them. The chickens would eat anything shiny. They would eat broken glass. They would eat broken light bulbs all the time. I always thought it would be a lucky day for the person at the chicken plant that found those chickens that had eaten the rings when they went to be slaughtered. Everything they ate you could find in the chicken's gizzard.

After my dad and J. C. got into it, we moved to town to some apartments that were ok except for the bathroom and kitchen, if you could even call it a kitchen. It was pretty hideous. J. C. was one of those kinds of people that had to have his way. Everything was about him. He was easily offended and it was really hard to always say and do what he wanted. You might say or do something one day and it would be ok. The next time you might get slapped or grounded like a kid.

A TRUE TRAGEDY: MY 9-11

My dad was still attending AA meetings. There was a big meeting coming up that you brought your family to. They would have a covered dish meal. My dad wanted me to go. My parents, and both of my sisters were going and I ask J. C. about us going. Of course, he was not going to go and neither was I. I could not believe that I was not going to be able to go to something so important with my family. I never would tell anybody why I couldn't do something. I was too afraid of him. He was going somewhere else with one of his buddies. I begged and pleaded with him to let me go. This was a special night for my dad. He had been sober for five years by this time. I felt a lot of pressure from my dad so I went anyway. I was too embarrassed to tell my parents that I was not allowed to go.

J. C. came back and found me gone is how he knew that I went. I think that he probably watched me after he had left for the night to see if I left. He came home around 3:00 or 4:00 in the morning. He dragged me out of the bed and beat up on me and slung me all over the apartment. I ran all over the apartment screaming trying to get away. Neighbors that I had never met came by the next day and introduced themselves to us. I am sure they came by, either out of concern to see if I was ok or they were just being nosy. Family was all I had.   If my parents or his parents made him mad, then I couldn't go around them or talk to them. I was only allowed to do things with certain family members at certain times.

I spent a lot of time with his grandmother and the neighbor across the street. I wasn't allowed to have friends at all. I was never allowed to do anything with any friends that I went to school with starting the day after we were married. We moved from the apartment in town to a trailer next to my in-laws. I continued to work for my mother at the restaurant. He decided that we were going to get pregnant. I had really bad morning sickness for the first few months. I took medication for morning sickness or I would not have been able to get out of bed or go to work. I worked for my mother until two weeks before my daughter was born.

I remember in the very beginning of my pregnancy I was really sick and my mother-in-law lived next door. I told J. C. to go and see if she had some Pepto-Bismol, because I was extremely sick. He never went, so I asked him if he was going to go get it for me. His response was that I told him to go instead of asking him; I didn't tell him to do anything. If I needed anything, I was supposed to say, "Would you *please* do something for me."

One night when I was pregnant, he was gone almost the entire night and when he got home, I asked him where he had been. I got the dog crap slapped out of me. He told me that I am not ever to ask him ever again where he was at. It was none of my business. He never went to the doctor with me. He had never, in the 13.5 years we were married, gone to the grocery store with me. He never kept the girls for me to do anything by myself, not one single time. We never went out to eat. We only ate at a fast-food restaurant about two times during the marriage, except for our honeymoon and two trips out of town. Never ate anywhere while we were dating, either. I was so sick once with a stomach bug. I was throwing up and couldn't hold my head up. I asked him if he would watch the girls for me so I could lie down. He would not; he left with his buddy and stayed gone all night.   He didn't go with me to the hospital when our first child had her tonsils taken out.

Back to when I was pregnant, I had gone past my due date by two weeks, so the doctor was going to induce labor. I was in labor for several hours. I had strong contractions for several hours and was in a lot of pain. I was only 19 and back then they didn't tell you a lot about what was going on. I was really not prepared for what I was about to experience. I gave birth to a beautiful Red Head. She had that beautiful red hair, and blue eyes. I was shocked over that also. All of my family members were blonde. Most of the red hair came from his side of the family. He had brown hair but a red beard. I was in the hospital for four days. We came home from the hospital. I was really excited because I thought now that we had this baby, things would be different. All I ever wanted was a family. I had these delusions that when I got married that somehow, I thought it was going to be like the Brady Bunch, I guess. He brought us home from the hospital and unloaded my things, then he left with one of his friends on motorcycles and was gone for three days. No cell phones back then. Couldn't call him; just had to sit and wait.

I quit working after I had my daughter. I spent a lot of time with my mother at the restaurant. I would go pick up supplies for her. I would also keep my youngest sister. She was eight years older than my daughter. They played together a lot. Things rocked on and, two years later, I was pregnant with my 2nd child. She, by the way, had piercing blue eyes and dark hair. No blonde hair like all my other cousins. I had kind of dirty blonde hair; my two sisters were cotton- tops.

By this time, my in-laws divorce; we bought their house from them. Sometime after we had moved in, I had started having problems sleeping. I started thinking that something was going to happen to someone very close to me. I was afraid that one of my girls was going to die. It was such a heavy burden that I went and met with my pastor. He tried to convince me that it was just other things going on in my life that were causing me to have those feelings. I knew that someone was going to die. I was so afraid that it would be one of my daughters that I would get up multiple times during the night to see if they were breathing.

During this time, my brother-in-law had come over for a little while to visit before heading out for a night on the town. He had to go by his dads to get the deposit from the business he was supposed to take to the bank. He had several thousands of dollars with him. He stopped by to visit some people that we went to school with so he didn't make it to the bank in time. They shared some of the conversations they had with him while he was there with me.

Later on that night, after midnight—during the wee hours of the morning—we received a phone call from the police department asking us if we were related to my brother-in-law. They had first been over to my father-in-law's, and couldn't get anyone to the door. That is why they showed up at our house. That is when they broke the news to us that he had been killed. He had left a bar that he was at and evidently passed out and hit a tractor trailer truck head on. They collided on a bridge and his car burst into flames.

I almost didn't think I could take it. I couldn't believe it. I knew then that was what I had been struggling with for months. My only regret was that I didn't take the opportunity that night to say some things that I had wanted to share with him. My pastor knew that my fears were real and not just stress. Sometime we get so caught up in our own fears of what we think is going to happen, that we miss opportunities that are right in front of us.

I had hoped his death would be an eye opener but the first thing that some of them did was pop open a can of beer as soon as we got home from the funeral. I couldn't believe it. I had hoped that would open J. C.'s eyes to the fact that life is short and he was headed down a primrose path of destruction.

J. C. had started working for an ice cream company. His uncle got him the job. He was making a lot of money. He made me starch and iron his shirts every day. I also was supposed to make them stay white somehow. Those two things took me back. Starched clothes and yellow whites. We still had well water and the shirts turned yellow after you washed them. We were really doing well financially. That all came to an end about as soon as it started. He was let go from the ice cream company. Seems he was stealing from one of the grocery stores. I think he was charging them for more ice cream than he was leaving. I always wondered why he brought so much ice cream home. He had a story for that also. I was so blind, like a child. I guess I believed everything I was told

I think that was about the time that his dad set him up a game room business at his convenience store that he owned. That didn't last long because it became a drinking and gambling business more than video game business. Not a lot of video game playing going on. He was the one that was doing most of the gambling and drinking. During the time he had the game room me and the girls had to move over there for a couple of months to take care of his dad because he had been shot and robbed.

One night, J. C. came in after the game room had closed. We were already asleep. My youngest daughter was in the bed with me and my oldest was asleep on a twin bed. J. C. was so drunk that he obviously had no idea where he was and what he was doing. He started peeing all over me and my daughter. I have never been so disgusted in all my life. That's what drugs and alcohol will do to a person. When you don't even know that you are peeing on someone asleep in the bed and you are not even aware of what you are doing. That is messed up. That was one of the sickest and grossest feelings that I had ever experienced in my life. The game room was losing money instead of making money.

This is about the time that my youngest daughter started doubling over with severe stomach pain. I took her to the doctor for about a year before we found out what was wrong. I thought she needed a companion because her sister had started school. I bought her a puppy, but that didn't help. I couldn't go out of the room out of her sight. I carried her around on my hip all the time. If I started out of the room without her, she would grab my leg and not let go. To make a long story short, the doctor found out she had stomach ulcers. She was on medication for a few years, even after she started to school. When she would see the school bus coming down the road, she would start throwing up. I would have to take her to school. I found out from her after a long time had passed that she did not want to leave me because she was afraid, I would die.

This is when he decided to get into the trucking business. He started driving for a company out of Birmingham. Of course, he had to own his own truck. His dad was always the one that helped him do everything that he wanted to do. He always fronted the money. J. C. was a very demanding person. He had to have his way or he would just cut you off if you didn't do what he wanted. That is how he controlled everyone in the family. You never knew what might make him mad. He would take revenge out on people.

I think he killed someone once. I never thought about that at the time. Many years later when I was thinking back on all the things that happened, I felt like that is what happened to this guy. I don't even remember his name or the year that this took place. I know the town and about the year that it took place.

I received a phone call from a stranger one night. He had information for me including pictures of J. C. and another girl together. He was trying to blackmail J. C. into giving him marijuana or he was going to release this information to me. I am not sure why the guy told me this before getting on the phone with J. C. He got on the phone with him and told him to just go right ahead and reveal the information to me. I really don't know what was said between the two of them. That's just what he said.

A couple of days later, J. C. came home and asked me if I remembered the guy that I talked to on the phone that was trying to blackmail him. Of course, I remembered. He said "well he is dead." They found him in the garage where he lived. He had hung himself. Years later as I have reflected back on the incident, in my own mind I believed he must have killed him. He was that mean. You will be convinced of the same thing by the time you get to the end of this book.

THE WRECK

This guy that graduated with my sister worked for the sheriff's department. He later became the sheriff where we lived. This incident happened when he was still a deputy. J. C. was out doing what he does best. Committing criminal activity, and up to no good. They had been looking for him for something else and so they blue-lighted him. That is all it took. It was on now. A high-speed chase began. The police lost him. He had outrun them.

He shows up at home and tells me what just happened. He was loving every minute of it. He decides to go out and find them and start the chase back up. This is a grown man that has no regard for other people's lives or his own for that matter. I pleaded with him to not go back out. Most men would be home with their wife and children. I think that he thought nothing would ever happen to him. Of course, it didn't for a long time. By then many other people's lives were damaged or almost totally destroyed.

He left and found the police and started the chase again. He took them down a dirt road that he was familiar with—a road that they were not. It was a dirt road, a road near our house. The dust was flying. I am sure you couldn't see 2 inches in front of them. This was a road that had a very large oak tree sitting very close to the road in a curve. He knew it was there. They did not. The two officers hit the tree as they turned the corner. The driver who was the guy that graduated high school with my sister had only minor injuries. The passenger's injuries were life threatening. The officer had major head trauma and multiple other injuries. He almost died.

J. C. came home and we left town for a few days until things cooled down. We stayed with my father-in-law's lady friend at the time in another town in Alabama. She didn't like us staying there and I didn't like being there. The girls were small and she didn't want them to mess up anything in her house. I don't blame her; I would feel the same way. My father-in-law did whatever he always did to get him out of trouble. I am not sure what he did but I know he got him out of a lot of trouble that he got himself in, whether it was financial or something else.

We came home when it was safe to return home. J. C.'s life continued on as usual. The injured officer's life was over as he knew it. He had brain damage and was crippled.

He was in a wheel chair and was unable to work anymore. The sheriff's department let him fill out police reports at the station. He could do small things like that. His life was ruined.

I remember thinking what would happen to J. C. for that. I wondered what would be the consequences for his actions. I wondered if my girls and I would suffer greatly for what he had caused in those people's lives. I grew up being taught that you pay for what you do. What goes around comes around. Other people also suffer for what others do. Everybody has a payday one day.

I had the opportunity to talk to the officer that didn't get hurt—and later became sheriff. He was later a volunteer at the TV station that I worked for many years later. He confirmed everything that I knew to be true. I don't know why nothing legally happened to J. C. I guess they couldn't prove it. I also think that the dirt road they were on turns into another county before you get to the end of it. I guess, where the accident happened, they had already crossed over the county line and was out of jurisdiction

THE RIG

The first Rig that he had broke down, and he wasn't going to pay to have it fixed for whatever reason. His main goal was to steal from you or beat you out of something. I am aware of a lot of things that he stole from other people. I know that he stole chains and other things off the back of other Rigs. This was probably in 1986 or 87. He took another truck out to California and left his at home sitting in the driveway.

The driveway was very close to our bedroom, where the backdoor was. Our bedroom was a closed-in carport. The girls went in and out of that door all the time to go out and play. They had been riding their bicycles out there most of the morning. We heated with propane gas. The large gas tank was out there as well. The girls had come into the house for a snack for a little while and, all of a sudden, I heard a crackling noise. I didn't think much about it until I had a frantic knock at the door. The person on the other side of the door was a passerby and saw the 18-wheeler truck was on fire. I couldn't believe my eyes. The fire department was called and they came and put it out. Keep in mind that my children could have been killed or injured if they had been out there and the truck had blown up, or the propane tank had blown up.

I called him out in California to let him know what had happened. He called the insurance company from California. The adjuster came out and spoke with me and I told him all that I knew. When he got home, the insurance adjuster came over several times. Their conversations all took place outside. J. C. told me that they were accusing him of setting it on fire. I couldn't believe they were accusing him of that. I was so naive. Stupid might be the correct word. He won the argument and he received the insurance money. I am sure that he threatened him and the agent was afraid. Everyone was afraid of him.

A TRUE TRAGEDY: MY 9-11

A few years after he had died, my brother-in-law said that J. C. got him to set the truck on fire to collect the insurance. I am sure he was afraid not to do it. Everyone who knew him was afraid of him.

He partied all the time. He had people over all the time. I called a lot of them his drinking buddies. One time he was having a party out at the barn and I saw girls going in out there. It was understood that I was never allowed out there. That was very upsetting to not know what was going on. I decided I couldn't take it and I was going out there. I was taking a big risk in doing this, but I did anyway. I thought I would take my chances. I knocked on the door and of course I was made a fool out of in front of everyone. I was told that I had better not ever do that again. I went back to the house with my two little girls and my tail between my legs. I knew not to ever go out there again when his friends were around.

J. C. never stayed at home. He was always drinking and out all hours of the night. I always left him a plate of food out to eat whenever he would come in. This night I was sick of making sure he had everything he needed at his fingertips. I decided not to leave his supper out for him because he might show up and he might not. That of course was a mistake. He came in around 3:00 or 4:00 in the morning and wanted to know where his food was. I said that I was tired of leaving it out or something to that effect. He threw the table over, picked up a chair and started beating it into the wall. My youngest daughter came out of the bedroom from all of the noise. The metal chair leg came close to going into her head. It would have killed her had that of happened. He just stopped and started toward me. I think that is the first time that I really thought I was going to die. I peed all over myself. That is the first time that I had ever lost control of my bodily functions. He pushed me into the microwave oven door so hard that I couldn't move my shoulder or arm. He made me clean up the gallon of spilt milk and turned over the table and would not let me go to the doctor. He warned me of what would happen if I said anything to anyone.

Years later, I ran into a guy that we went to school with. He told me that J. C. was so mean that, when we were in school, one thing that he did when they were out riding around was to plug a spotlight into his cigarette lighter. When he would meet a car, he would shine the spot light in their eyes and cause them to run off the road. He also would throw beer bottles at people walking down the road and hit them with the bottles. I never knew about this. I mainly only knew about the things that he did to me.

I was at my 40th class reunion and a guy that I graduated with talked to me about how mean and afraid of him everybody was. He said that they were at this guy's house one night he bought beer from. He said that J. C. was furious and came after them for not buying from him. He said that he started chasing after him and J. C. tripped over a case of beer and fell. He said that, had he not fallen, he didn't know what would have happened to him. There was one person that was not afraid of him. That was my dad. I wish I could say, one more time, "Thank you, daddy."

My brother-in-law told me that he was with him one time out on the road in his rig. J. C. had hired this prostitute. While he was outside of the rig, she stole money out of his wallet. He said that he beat the crap out of her. He could steal from you all day long, but you had better not steal from him.

METH ADDICTION

While traveling to California in his rig, J. C. decides to take us with him. I have no idea why. We went out there and back in nine days. While we were there, we went to the truck stop that he hung out at when he would take loads out there. I found out later that our waitress at the truck stop was his girlfriend. I guess he wanted her to meet his children. I am sure there was a motive. I am not sure what it was. I have given it a little thought but not a lot. I just have to speculate.

California is where he was introduced to the drug Meth. Once while he was on a trip to California, I got a call from the hospital while he was out there that he had collapsed while unloading his truck. He had overdosed on drugs. This is the first time that I had heard of Meth. It was what a lot of truck drivers in the 80's called crank. Now called "crack." The medical people said this was a new drug, and that recovery was little to none.

He came home and checked into a rehab. He was only there a few days before he pulled a screwdriver on the staff demanding that they let him out. I wanted to know how he got the screwdriver to use as a weapon. He had taken it off the pool table that a maintenance man had accidentally left there. The girls and I were at a Carmen concert with our church group, only to come home and find out he had left the recovery center. This was such a disappointment. Little did I know how big a disappointment this was going to turn out to be.

This was in the 80's and Meth was not popular in the south at that time. He was immediately addicted to Meth as most people are after the first time they try it. J. C. decided that he is going to try and make Meth himself and sell it. He used all kinds of household chemicals to try and create this drug. He used anything and everything including rat poison and bleach. Once again, the girls and I had to leave our home while he played the mad scientist.

My sister and her husband lived in a trailer on our property. The trailer was next door to our house. We stayed with her for about two or three months. He was ok with us leaving; believe you me when I say this. It was on his terms, and our lives were in danger from breathing the fumes from all the chemicals that he was cooking on the stove and in the microwave oven. He even blew up the microwave oven. He ruined all of my stainless-steel cookware and silverware. He ruined our refrigerator. He finally gave up on that. You can easily make Meth now. I think they call it "shake and bake." People still blow themselves up today making Meth.

Toward the end, he became very paranoid and put coverings on all the windows and closed off all the rooms. He was sure people were watching him. Little did I know that I would be putting coverings on all the windows to protect myself from him.

He got on the needle and I made him swear that my daughters would never see him shoot up. One day one of the girls did see it. After that she would sit in the corner a lot when he was there and she would keep her distance from him.

If it was illegal and you could make money doing it, you could count him in. He couldn't make an honest living if his life depended on it. He fought chickens and pit bulldogs. He even raised fighting chickens at our house for a period of time. He made me feed them when he wasn't there. It hurt my heart to look at those chickens and to know the torture they were about to experience. All my life growing up, we killed chickens for food. That death is instant and used for food. These chickens had sharp things on their heads or feet and they fought until one was dead or both.

I saw it one time when another guy came to our house and brought his chickens to our house. I also saw two dogs fight. I had to walk away; it was so inhumane. He had no compassion or misery for suffering inflicted on others. To think of someone inflicting something that brutal on an animal was more than I could take. I wish I had never looked. Some things that you see in life you wished your eyes had never seen.

He also bootlegged for a while. I remember one time that someone gave him a head's up that he was about to be raided for illegal alcohol sales. He started pouring everything out and getting rid of his evidence. By the time they got there it was too late. They knew what he had done, but there was nothing to arrest him on.

I continued to take my girls to church. I did a lot of church work. One time he told me I couldn't go but I did anyway. We left so quick that one of the girls didn't have on shoes. There was no consequence that day for disobeying. I'm not sure why.

His sexual activity became weird and excessive. When he was there, I had to have sex with him sometimes five times a day. I couldn't be gone long anywhere because he might want sex. I had started the girls in piano lessons. This particular day I was taking them for their lesson which lasted only an hour. I was ordered to take and drop them off and return immediately back home because he couldn't wait that long for his sexual ritual. I have been told that is why a lot of children who live with or are around someone addicted to Meth are sexually abused. The reason is that drugs cause a person to have that uncontrollable craving.

He had this ritual that he started doing before sex. He was on the needle and he had to shoot up each time right before he had sex. He started wanting to watch young girls on video's having sex right before.

He was having trouble at this point getting the satisfaction that he needed. He had to do more and more weird things. His rituals were becoming more and more sick. I began to wonder what he was really doing. The thought of him actually doing something with a young girl after seeing the video scared me to death.

He had this chest that he would bring into the house. I didn't know what was in it. One day he went outside and I thought I would have time to look in the chest. I looked and there was a blowup doll in there along with x rated videos and a few other items. I got sick to my stomach. I can only image what you do with a blowup doll. Shortly after the girls started piano lessons, I had to make them quit because I didn't have the money for them to continue. It's funny how the piano lessons never played out for me or them.

EVENTS LEADING UP TO 9-11

J. C. had been gone for a while. I have no idea where he was. He was gone a few days. He came home this particular night and told me that he was going to burn the house down and collect the insurance. He told me that I needed to get everything out. He also told me about his affair that he had been having with this waitress that he met in California.

He had only been taking work from our county that would be going back to California and back to where we lived because he would bring his girlfriend back with him. Sometimes it took six weeks to get a load going to California, and back to Cullman. Sometimes he would be gone that long and I would not hear a word from him. Sometimes he would call and check in.

When he would bring her home with him, he would come home and take a shower and stay about 30 minutes and leave and stay gone a couple of days before he would come back home. My father-in-law was letting her stay at his house and J. C. would go over there and stay with her. He did that routine until he would get another load back to California. J. C. and his girlfriend would then travel back to California. I guess the hardest thing to swallow was to think that my father-in-law would have shown that much disrespect to me and his own granddaughters allowing him to bring another woman to hide out at his home so he could be with this girl.

I never knew about her until that night. I don't know her name or anything about her. He told me how in love he was with her and that he was going to leave me for her, but he loved me and decided he wanted to stay with me. My guess is that she saw the light and dumped him. I was all that was left. I'm guessing she stayed in California, "smart girl." I have also wondered if she was even alive. Maybe she no longer existed. Maybe I was all that was left.

He leaves and says that he will be back. I knew that he had really lost it at this point. I never felt so betrayed in all my life. I had never been with another man but J. C. I took my marriage vows seriously. I can't describe how I felt. I felt like a part of me had been given to that other woman. I felt like the most personal thing about me had been shared with another person. I felt like someone else was a part of my flesh and soul. I knew he was a cheater, but actually hearing it I knew it for sure. I felt disgusted.

I did a test on him once. I heard it on a talk show, how to give your spouse a test if you think they are cheating. They said that, if your husband was a cheater, when he would come home from work or a trip and would immediately start a fight, get mad and leave, that was a good sign. He passed the test with flying colors. Now that I look back, that is what he was doing the entire time that he was bringing his girlfriend back to Alabama. She would be at his dads and he would start a fight with me so he could leave.

I was very afraid of him. I didn't know when he would be back or how long he would be gone. I called my mother and told her that I was in a great deal of danger. This was around 2am in the morning when all this took place. She told me to start packing and she would be over there at daylight with a trailer to start moving me out. We moved all day long. I had no money, only one shiny dime in my purse.

My parents had found this house for me to rent that was close to them. I needed $600.00 to move in. Three hundred for deposit and $300.00 for the first month's rent. As we were leaving my home where we had lived around 10 years with our last load of belongings, I made one last trip to the mail box and there was a check in there. The check was a refund from the homeowner's insurance from the previous year. Somehow too much had been paid. It was exactly what I needed to move into this house. I once again am trying to process this in my mind. This was another sign of protection from God.

It didn't take long for him to find me. I guess he thought I would be at my parents and he would see my car there. He also was in the area because he was hanging out with one of his uncles who lived in the area. I guess it was pretty shocking when he came back home to find nothing there but his desk and a towel that belonged to him. After all he did tell me to take everything out of the house. He didn't burn the house down but, little did I know, that flames were soon approaching.

I got a job at a restaurant in town. My dad had to follow me to and from work every day because I was being stalked and harassed by him. During the time leading up to my 9-11, I had been home from work only a few minutes and I heard a noise, the same noise that I had heard before. It was that crackling noise that I heard when the Tractor trailer rig was engulfed in flames. I suddenly had a flash back. I ran to the window and to my surprise my car was burnt to the ground. Another scare tactic to let me know he was in control, and that I would have to do what he said. I found out that I couldn't do anything legally about the burned-up car. I found out that you could burn up your own car as long as you didn't try to collect insurance. The car didn't have my name on it. I am pretty sure it was in his dad's name because that is where the car came from. He had a small used car lot at his business. He wasn't going to do anything to his own son for that.

I had to go buy a pay by the week car. I had to pay $600.00 down and $116.00 a month total. My sister loaned me $500.00 and my dad $100.00. I paid back every penny that I borrowed from my dad and sister. I have never owed anyone for long.

These two-gentleman pulled up shortly after the car fire; I had not been home from work long. They were investigators. They were asking me if I knew where J.C. was. I didn't of course. At first, they didn't believe me. They thought that I was protecting him like most women do, especially abused women. My abuse was more mental, and brainwashing; it was major control with a little physical abuse thrown in when I was least expecting it. Some of it was abuse to humiliate you in front of other people. Once we were playing cards with his mother and her husband. I made a comment about the card game. I don't remember what it was, but it was something normal to say. He didn't like it so he grabbed me by the hair of the head and jerked my hair so hard. No one said a word. No one knew what to say. The game ended quickly.

They were looking for him. I told them that I was looking for him also. He had just recently burned up my car and I wanted him arrested. I had a protection order against him but we all know that doesn't stop fists or bullets. It is a paper trail, and that is what will save you in the end. That is the most important thing you need to do in a situation like I was in. They then realized that I was on their side and that I needed someone on my side. The reason they were looking for him was he had stolen a brand-new flatbed trailer.

Another time he came over, busted the front door in, and told me he was taking the girls for a ride. They did not want to go. They were very afraid of him. I told him over my dead body. The one thing is, when it came to my girls, I didn't care what he did to me as long as he didn't touch them.

It was almost over my dead body for sure. He picked up the dining table glass top, threw it down and broke it into a million pieces. Then he came after me. He picked me up by the neck with his hands. He held me up against the wall with my feet dangling and was trying to choke me. Then he started trying to beat my head into the bathroom sink. He all of a sudden just stopped. He told me to start packing my things—I was not going to get a divorce and leave him. He said he would be back.

He left, and the girls came running back into the house. They had run across the road and hid behind the neighbor's house. They thought I was dead. I ask them when they were adults had their dad ever tried to do anything inappropriate because of an incident that had happened with a family member. They said, "No." If he had been able to leave with them that day and had taken them for a ride, something bad might have happened. He had previously gotten them into the big truck; he starting playing with one of the girls' hair and telling her that she was his girl. She felt that, if he had of been able to leave with them, something would have happened.

THE SHERIFF

Things are to the point that I have to do something if I want to survive. When I moved over close to my parents, I was in a different county. I actually was right on the county line. Power was provided by one county and water from the county I just came from.

I decided I needed some protection from Law enforcement. I decided to go to the Sheriff's Department. They could pick him up if they came across him and I also got a protection order against him. All of those things you will need to do to protect yourself legally if anything happens to you—like it did me. We all know that a piece of paper doesn't stop bullets or fists, but it will help protect you in a court of law. You need to file a report for every single incident.

In the late 80's was about the time things started to change for the better for abused women. A lot of women went to prison for killing their abuser because they never filed a report. One of the reasons a person would not file a report is because it would make things a lot worse for you especially if you are living with your abuser. You are also made to feel guilty and like it's your fault. They make you feel sorry for them not sorry for what they have done to you. It was hard for me but easier too because I had the support of my dad. I also knew that he would not help me at all if I went back.

I was given advice from the authorities that it would be in my best interest to get myself some protection. I told them there was no way I could shoot a gun. They asked me if I was going to just stand by and let someone kill me and my children. I told them I guess I was. That is how big a coward I am. I got a gun and target practiced with it. I would never use it.

I also found out that day that if you are married to someone they have as much right to take your children and leave with them as you do and there is nothing you can do about it. I am not sure if the laws are still the same today but that was the law in 1989.

ATTORNEY

They told me the only way to protect my children was to file for divorce. The big D! That is what I had always been taught by my mother that is something you did not do. The words played over in my mind—that if I didn't stay with him, I would somehow be responsible if he never turned his life over to the Lord. My mother reveals to me that she doesn't care anymore. Sounds horrible to say but Thank You Jesus!! Our safety is what is important now. I really didn't know who to go to.

I wanted to go to the county that I was from. My dad knew a man that had been an attorney and a Judge. I called that office and they gave me an appointment. My mother and I walk in not knowing what to expect. I encounter a very pleasant lady with a beautiful smile who is going to help me. I proceeded to tell her my story. This is the beginning of hope that I had not had before. She gave me hope. I felt like there was a light at the end of the tunnel. She writes up a divorce agreement and I sent word to him by his dad that he needed to meet me at the attorney's office. I was pretty sure that he would not show up. I get to the appointment and he showed up. I was trembling all over my body. He read the agreement and of course refused to sign anything.

There was an ice cream shop next door. We went in there to talk. He was not agreeing to anything and that I would do what he said. He started getting very verbal and I walked out. I was so distraught and, in a hurry, to get to work that I was almost hit by a car or should I say more than one car. I walked out into oncoming traffic on Highway 31. That is when I just had to do this on my own. I was getting a divorce with or without him. He was not going to take the girls anywhere. Once again it would be over my dead body. I didn't know at the time how true those words would be.

Today is 9-11-1989. The time had come to go to my attorney's office and sign my divorce papers. My attorney ran an ad in the newspaper for the allotted time, saying that we did not know his whereabouts at the time—which we didn't. So, the day had arrived for me to sign the paperwork for me to be divorced without his signature. All that was left to do was to get the paper work signed by a judge and my divorce would be final

By this time, I am emotionally and physically drained. I had not one ounce of strength left in my body. I went to my mother's and I told her I was ready to die. I couldn't take it anymore. The stress and pain were too much. I knew he was going to kill me and I told my mother that I couldn't fight anymore. There is a part of you that thinks it's going to happen, and a part of you that tells you that, no, this can't really happen. My mother said no, no!!! You have to be strong.

I went home and when evening came, I ask my dad if he would stay at my house that night. We would have either spent the night with my parents, or my dad would have stayed with us. At that time my parents had been living in a single wide trailer. I was renting a small house from a lady less than a mile down the road from my parents. The house was what they called a valley home. I really didn't want to stay with my parents because I would have to sleep on the floor. I was very tired, and wanted to sleep in my own bed. I was working about 17 hours a day. I worked as a waitress, and I also cleaned houses and ironed for this couple that I went to church with. I had never been so broke in all my life. I was struggling to make ends meet. I didn't even have enough money to buy a soft drink out of a machine that costs less than .50 cents.

9-11

My dad came to stay for the night like he had many times before. This time he brought his hand gun and shotgun. Shortly after my dad arrived, the phone calls began. J. C. had been calling and threatening me on a daily basis. This particular night he told me he was going to kill himself and he was taking me and the girls with him. He said that there was going to be bloodshed tonight. My dad took the phone from me and told him that, if he tried to touch me one more time, he would have to go through him first.

After my dad got off the phone with J. C., I wanted to start covering the windows with sheets. The windows had mini blinds on them, but they were cheap and would not close all the way. You could still see through them. I was afraid that he would try and shoot me through the window while I was sleeping. My dad didn't think that was necessary, but I did it anyway. He had come to the window before when I was asleep at night.

I had been letting the girls take turns sleeping with me and it was the youngest daughter's turn that night. I decided not to let her because I was afraid, he would try and shoot me through the window and she might get shot. We all got ready for bed. I always had Bible devotion with the girls every night and had God's prayer of protection over us. My dad was going to sleep on the sofa and he always went to sleep as long as I remember my entire adult life watching TV.

For some reason he wanted the TV off. I questioned him because it was so out of the ordinary. He said that he was tired and just wanted to go to sleep. I know now that was just one more of God's way of protecting us and sparing our lives. Had there been any light coming in from the TV shining in the house the story would have turned out differently.

I remember lying in the bed just a few days before sick to my stomach thinking it was really going to happen. One minute I would feel like I knew that I was going to die. Then I would feel like, "No! This won't really happen. There was no way that he would really kill us, would he?" I had thought about us trying to leave and never be found. I didn't think that we could really pull that off. Where would we go and how would we survive.

We all go to bed and all the lights are off except the bathroom light. I always left the bathroom light on. Till this day, there is a light still burning in my house that is never turned off. I was so tired that I fell right asleep. At 10:55 p.m., the telephone rang. This is when we only had a land line. There was a strange scratchy unrecognizable voice on the other end saying, "Who is this?" I said, "Julie." They said, "Who," and hung up the phone. I got up and went to the bathroom and did something that I have never done before in my life. I turned out the light. I have no idea why I did it. I even turned around to turn it back on, and said to myself, "Why did I turn that light out?" I was so tired that I didn't want to think about it, so I laid right back down. Just another of God's hedges of protection over us.

The only thing you could see was a tiny green dot on the microwave oven. Back then, microwave ovens were very large and heavy. They had a little tiny light that stayed on all the time. The light was no larger than the end of an ink pen. I went back to bed, and immediately went back to sleep. The police said that I called for help at 11:13 p.m. Back in 1989, we didn't have 9-11; we dialed "0" for the operator.

The next thing I heard a blast. I didn't know what I was hearing until I heard a voice saying, "Where are you at?" He was calling out my dad's name. I started running, and almost most ran into him. I was trapped, with nowhere to go. As my body almost touched his—POW!! He fired again, grazing the side of my head with the pellets from the sawed-off shotgun. I knew I was trapped with no way out. I turned around and ran into my oldest daughter. I ran back to my bedroom; I heard another shot and then silence. I remember just standing there in the dark and my youngest daughter screaming and wouldn't stop. She said she thought we were dead. She said she couldn't move her body. She was frozen.

At that time, I didn't know where my oldest daughter was because I had run into her and thought she ran back with me to the bedroom. I remember I heard a noise that sounded like rain dripping off the gutter of a house. I found out later that it was J. C. It was the sound of a person gurgling.   I spoke; I said, "Who's there?" Suddenly, my dad spoke and said, "It's J. C. I shot him." About that time, my daughter came running back into the house. She was covered in blood. I didn't know if she had been shot. I also didn't know that I was bleeding on the side of my head. I took her and sat her down on the floor beside her sister and dialed the operator. I ask her, "Where did you go?" She said she was going to get in the car and drive away. When my youngest daughter had heard my voice, she stopped screaming and was able to move. She thought everyone was dead.

My two girls were just nine and eleven years old when this happened on 9-11-1989. I made sure the eleven-year-old was ok. I didn't clean her up until after the police got there. My dad remained standing in the same spot holding his gun until the police and ambulance arrived. He didn't know if J. C. was still alive and might fire his gun again.

What had happened was that, when I had turned around and ran into my daughter after he had fired and blown a hole in the wall behind me the size of a basketball, she hadn't turned around and gone back toward the bedroom. She had kept going and run into her dad. He was leading my daughter out of the door with the gun held to her head. He didn't have on a shirt. He had a hand gun strapped to his shoulder and a sawed-off shotgun that he had blew the door in with. When he blew the door in, the outside light was shining in enough that my dad could see him. J. C. had still not seen my dad, until my dad spoke as he was going out the door with my daughter and said, "Turn her loose." My dad actually thought he was holding me. J. C. then turned toward my dad and fired his gun. My dad fired shooting him in the side and the bullet going through the lungs.

The investigator said that J. C.'s gunned jammed is the reason that he wasn't able to shoot my dad first. J. C.'s last words were, "You son-of-a-bitch!!!" And he stumbled out the door and fell. The ambulance people arrived and started CPR.

After calling the police, I called my friend that I cleaned and ironed for. She and her husband had been praying for me. I had also gone to church with them for years. She rushed over there as fast as she could. She told me years later that she remembers every single minute of what happened that night. She said that when she got there she saw J. C. lying on the ground, making the same noise that I had heard, and when she got to me, she had never seen anyone in the shape that I was in. She grabbed me and held onto me tight. She told me that during that entire time that I was going through everything with J. C. that she didn't know if I was going to make it. She said, "I was just surviving minute- to-minute."

I found out later that J. C.'s uncle (that was only four years older than he) was the driver. He brought him over to where I was living, was instructed by J. C. (according to his police statement) to drive down the road to a certain place, turn around and come back and pick him up. I should have pressed charges against him. In my opinion he was an accomplice to the crime that was committed against us.

According to the police, he claimed that he didn't know that J. C. was planning on doing that. It is hard to believe that someone that is in the car with you and they don't have on a shirt, has a hand gun strapped to their shoulder, and has a sawed-off shotgun in their hand, and ask you to drive so far down the road and come back and pick you up, didn't know what was about to happen, "PLEASE!!!"

My dad and I were allowed to go back to my parents and clean up before going to the police station for a statement and fingerprints. I remember when I got to my parents' house, I had been okay up to that point. I then started to hyperventilate. I couldn't breathe. I guess reality of what had just happened set in. My parents got a brown paper bag and had me to breathe in it. My dad and I went to the police station and that is when they told me he had died.

The next day, I was staring out the window in disbelief of what had just taken place; both of my sweet girls were running and playing like normal, innocent children would. At that moment the fear of being taken or killed was gone. One of my children said that night they hoped that their dad died. The day after the other one said that she was glad he was dead.

I also was told by investigators, that the woman that J. C. had been hanging out with, who was also a meth user called J. C.'s father and told him what he was about to do. He told her to call him if anything happened. I think that he didn't think anything would happen. At least I hope that is what he thought. I have to think that he surely didn't think that someone could be killed—knowing that two little innocent girls that were his granddaughters' lives were at stake.

I also learned that the woman was going to testify before the Grand Jury hearing regarding the telephone conversion with J. C.'s father. I know that is true because I was sitting there when she walked right by me in shackles and chains on her way in to appear before the Grand Jury. I also learned that I would not have even had to go before the Grand Jury had one of his family members had not pushed it. The only reason she did it was because of whom she was married to. She thought she was really important because of her husband's position.

I was very nervous, because I had never experienced anything like this. We were not indicted. I found out later that a lot of people, some that were considered very important, came before the Grand Jury as character witnesses and had testified on our behalf. I was very thankful and grateful for all who did that for us.

I am sure that I will never get completely over what I experienced, but as time goes on, I feel stronger every day. I have experienced many night mares. In my night mares I am running and running in the dark, because I am being chased. When I am caught, I am being choked to death. Had it not been for my present husband, who would wake me up, I really believe I would have died as a result of my dreams. That is how traumatic and real my dreams were. I have many fears, things that scare me. I never had the counseling that I should have had. I only went a couple of times. I feel it is very important to seek counsel if you have the right kind. My saving grace was a friend of mine at my church prayed over me regarding my nightmares a few years ago. I got to thinking about that as I have been writing this book and realized that since that time, I have not had a full-blown nightmare. I was truly delivered from that.

THE END

ABOUT THE AUTHOR

JULIE WILHITE

Growing up in a small town in Alabama on a chicken farm was tough on a young girl in the early 60's, not to mention being a teenager in the 70's. It was not what most girls would envision their life to be like. Life was tough, but surviving all that went into the farm life and what I know now as an adult was somewhat a dysfunctional family life. It was way easier than the survival that I was about to face as an adult. My mother was a devoted Christian, homemaker and later became a nurse. My dad was a farmer. All of what I endured as a child prepared me for life, but at the same time played a big role in the decisions that I made, good and bad.

I married when I was young, and had two daughters. My faith in Jesus Christ is the reason I am able to tell my story today. I always knew that one day I would share events leading up to my 9-11 experience. After over 30 years have passed, I am writing this book hoping that other women will be encouraged by the events that took place in my life and my two daughters' life on 9-11-1989. I married my present husband nine years later. He has truly been a blessing from God.

Made in the USA
Columbia, SC
17 June 2024

36737273R00072